RAISING RESILIENT KIDS WITH ADHD

Strategies For Success

SHAWN TAYLOR

Table of Contents

CHAPTER ONE

Introduction

ADHD can make parenting difficult. ADHD impairs a child's concentration, impulse control, and hyperactivity, making daily tasks harder. However, ADHD children have great strengths and resilience.

"Raising Resilient Kids with ADHD - Strategies for Success" offers parents insights, practical advice, and effective strategies to support their children's development, well-being, and resilience. Parents can support growth, self-advocacy, and success by understanding ADHD.

This book offers parents practical strategies, real-life examples, and resources for raising ADHD-resilient children. Parents can help their children thrive, overcome challenges, and build a successful and fulfilling future by using these strategies and embracing their strengths.

CHAPTER TWO

Understanding ADHD

Adults and children alike can be affected by the neurodevelopmental disorder known as attention deficit hyperactivity disorder (ADHD). It is characterized by inattention, hyperactivity, and impulsivity that persist over time and have a negative impact on daily functioning and well-being.

Inattention and hyperactivity/impulsivity are the two most prominent hallmarks of attention deficit hyperactivity disorder. Symptoms of inattention include a lack of ability to maintain focus, a propensity for distraction, sloppiness, and a general lack of discipline. Symptoms of hyperactivity and impulsivity include incessant movement, difficulty sitting still, making snap judgments, speaking without thinking, and interrupting others.

Symptoms of attention deficit hyperactivity disorder (ADHD) can vary in intensity and presentation from one person to the next. Adults can also be affected by ADHD, though their symptoms may look different than they did when they were younger.

Types of ADHD

ADHD can be further classified into three main types:

Predominantly Inattentive Presentation (formerly known as ADD): Those of this type have more trouble paying attention than being hyperactive or impulsive. They often have trouble concentrating, daydream a lot, and have trouble with other aspects of executive functioning.

Predominantly Hyperactive-Impulsive Presentation: Hyperactivity and impulsivity are more pronounced in this subtype, while inattention may be less so. These people might fidget, have trouble sitting still, act rashly without thinking things through, and have trouble interacting with others.

Combined Presentation: Symptoms of inattention and hyperactivity/impulsivity coexist in this subtype. Individuals with this presentation of ADHD often struggle in a number of different areas and show a wide variety of ADHD symptoms.

Common Challenges Faced by Kids with ADHD

Challenges in daily functioning, school success, and social relationships are all real possibilities for children with ADHD. Among the most frequent difficulties are:

Academic difficulties: Young people with attention deficit hyperactivity disorder (ADHD) may have trouble paying attention in school, which can impact their ability to learn and succeed. Academic performance may suffer and self-esteem may suffer as a result.

Impaired executive functioning: Time management, organization, planning, and problem solving are all executive functions that can be impaired in those with ADHD. Because of these obstacles, it may be hard for children to finish projects, adhere to directions, and handle responsibilities responsibly.

Social and relationship issues: Due to impulsivity, hyperactivity, or trouble reading social cues, children with ADHD may struggle in group settings. Since they may have difficulty keeping friends, sharing, and controlling their feelings, they may withdraw socially and feel unwanted.

Emotional regulation: Children who suffer from ADHD may find it more difficult to control their feelings. They may have trouble regulating their emotions and finding ways to calm themselves down after experiencing strong reactions.

Impact of ADHD on Resilience

A child's resilience may be negatively affected by ADHD. Being resilient means you can deal with adversity and come out on top. While there are many factors that contribute to a child's level of resilience, ADHD can present additional challenges that make it more difficult for a child to overcome adversity.

Academic difficulties, impaired executive functioning, social difficulties, and emotional regulation issues are just some of the ways in which a child's resilience can be tested by ADHD. They may have to deal with adversity on a regular basis, encounter frustration, and get negative responses from those around them. Their sense of worth, drive, and confidence might all take a hit as a result.

It is critical, however, to acknowledge that children with ADHD also have innate strengths and resilience potential. They can learn the skills of resilience necessary to face adversity head-on, gain confidence in the face of adversity, and succeed in a variety of contexts if they are given the resources they need to do so.

Parents can play a pivotal role in developing their child's resilience by employing helpful strategies and providing a nurturing environment. This book is written for parents of children with attention deficit hyperactivity disorder (ADHD) and aims to give them tools to help their children thrive in spite of the difficulties they face.

CHAPTER THREE

Building a Supportive Environment

Children with ADHD require a nurturing setting in which they can flourish and build resiliency. Parents can help their children flourish by providing an atmosphere conducive to development, self-assurance, and health. Key components of a nurturing setting for children with ADHD are outlined below.

Creating a Structured Routine

Having a daily routine can be helpful for children with ADHD. Predictability and lower anxiety levels are two benefits of maintaining a regular routine.

Here are some tips for creating a structured routine:

- Set regular times for waking up, meals, homework, playtime, and bedtime.
- Use visual aids such as schedules, calendars, or timers to help children understand and follow the routine.
- Break tasks into smaller, manageable steps and incorporate regular breaks to improve focus and productivity.
- Be flexible and allow for adjustments, when necessary, but try to maintain a general routine to provide stability.

Parents can aid their children's attention deficit hyperactivity disorder (ADHD) by instituting routines that help them keep track of time, stay organized, and feel in charge of their day.

Establishing Clear Expectations

Children are less likely to experience confusion or frustration when they have a firm grasp on what is expected of them. Think about the following when setting expectations:

Establish and reiterate behavioral expectations in the home and in other environments.

Create concise, easy-to-follow directions for completing a project or chore.

Motivate and reward desired actions with positive reinforcement.

Help children keep on track by reminding them and prompting them occasionally.

Parents can aid their children with ADHD in developing self-discipline, understanding boundaries, and a sense of accomplishment through consistent and clear expectations.

Promoting Positive Communication

Building a friendly community begins with open lines of communication. It facilitates communication between parents and their ADHD children, allowing them to better address each other's concerns and needs.

Here are some strategies for promoting positive communication:

- Practice active listening by giving your child your full attention, maintaining eye contact, and showing empathy.

- Use clear and concise language when giving instructions or providing feedback.

- Encourage open and honest conversations, allowing your child to express their thoughts and feelings.

- Teach and model effective communication skills, such as using "I" statements and problem-solving techniques.

Parents can strengthen their relationship with their children, build trust and understanding, and encourage open dialogue by modeling these traits themselves.

Providing Emotional Support

Kids who struggle to control their feelings may have attention deficit hyperactivity disorder. With your help, they can learn to cope with adversity and manage their feelings. Think about implementing these tactics:

- Validate your child's feelings and emotions, letting them know it is okay to feel and express themselves.
- Teach and practice relaxation techniques, such as deep breathing or mindfulness exercises, to help manage stress and anxiety.
- Encourage the development of healthy coping mechanisms, such as engaging in hobbies or activities they enjoy.
- Foster a safe and non-judgmental environment where your child feels comfortable discussing their emotions and seeking support.

Parents can aid their children with ADHD in managing their emotions, strengthening their emotional resilience, and developing positive coping mechanisms by providing them with emotional support.

Collaborating with Schools and Educators

Working together with teachers and school administrators is crucial to developing a community of care that goes beyond the family unit.

Here are some ways to collaborate effectively:

- Share information about your child's ADHD diagnosis and any specific accommodations they may require.
- Establish open lines of communication with teachers, counselors, and other school staff to

exchange information and address concerns.

- Work together to develop an individualized education plan (IEP) or a 504 plan to outline necessary accommodations and support in the school setting.

- Attend parent-teacher meetings and actively participate in your child's education, offering insights and working collaboratively to address challenges.

Parents can help their child with attention deficit hyperactivity disorder (ADHD) succeed in school and in life by working together with teachers and other school staff.

Children with ADHD benefit greatly from the creation of a nurturing atmosphere.

Parents can give their children agency and a leg up in life by establishing routines, setting clear expectations, encouraging open lines of communication, providing emotional support, and working in tandem with teachers.

CHAPTER FOUR

Enhancing Self-Awareness and Self-Advocacy

Children with ADHD must learn to understand themselves and to advocate for themselves. These abilities equip them to advocate for themselves effectively and to evaluate their own circumstances in terms of their strengths, weaknesses, and specific requirements. In what follows, we'll look at ways to help kids with ADHD learn to advocate for themselves and become more self-aware.

Developing a Growth Mindset

Ability and intelligence are not fixed traits; rather, they can be cultivated through practice and experience. Children with ADHD benefit from developing a growth mindset because it encourages them to see setbacks less as barriers and more as opportunities for personal development. How parents can encourage a growth mindset is discussed below.

Instill a growth mindset by stressing the value of failure as a learning experience.

Instead of focusing solely on outcomes or achievements, praise effort, persistence, and strategies used.

Instruct young people to replace destructive inner monologue with more optimistic self-talk.

Make sure kids have plenty of chances to participate in activities that will help them develop and improve.

Children with ADHD can benefit from a more optimistic outlook, increased resilience, and a love of a challenge by adopting a growth mindset.

Helping Kids Understand their ADHD

Understanding ADHD is a crucial first step in teaching children to accept and manage their condition. Children can learn to effectively advocate for themselves and others with ADHD if they are given accurate information about the disorder.Consider the following strategies:

- Use age-appropriate language and explanations to help children understand what ADHD is and how it impacts their daily lives.
- Provide resources and books that explain ADHD in relatable and accessible ways.

- Encourage open conversations where children can ask questions and express their thoughts and feelings about their ADHD.
- Help children identify their strengths and unique abilities associated with ADHD.

Parental education about ADHD can help kids accept themselves as they are, take responsibility for their difficulties, and grow into confident adults.

Teaching Self-Regulation and Coping Skills

Children with ADHD need to learn to self-regulate and cope in order to control their feelings and behaviors. Parents can aid their children in developing self-control and coping strategies by teaching them these skills.. Consider the following strategies:

- Teach and practice mindfulness techniques, such as deep breathing or meditation, to help children calm their minds and bodies.

- Help children identify triggers that may lead to impulsive behaviors or emotional outbursts and teach them strategies to manage these triggers.

- Teach problem-solving skills, such as breaking down tasks, brainstorming solutions, and evaluating consequences.

- Encourage the use of visual cues or self-monitoring tools to promote self-awareness and self-regulation.

Parents can help their children with attention deficit hyperactivity disorder (ADHD) control their impulses and emotions and make better choices by teaching them self-regulation and coping skills.

Encouraging Self-Advocacy and Assertiveness

Self-advocacy is the skill of speaking up for one's own interests, standing up for one's rights, and expressing oneself clearly. Children with ADHD can benefit from learning to be their own advocates in school, in relationships, and in their own health and well-being if they are taught to do so. Think about implementing these tactics:

- Teach children to identify and communicate their strengths, challenges, and needs related to their ADHD.

- Role-play various situations to help children practice assertiveness and self-advocacy skills.

- Encourage children to ask for help when needed and provide guidance on how to approach teachers, peers, or other individuals for support.

- Foster a supportive environment where children feel comfortable expressing their thoughts, concerns, and preferences.

Parents can help their children with ADHD become more independent and self-reliant by teaching them to advocate for themselves, be assertive when asking for help, and take an active role in making decisions that affect their lives.

Children with ADHD can build resilience and achieve greater levels of success by improving their capacity for self-awareness and self-advocacy. Parents can equip their children to make the most of their strengths, overcome obstacles, and advocate for themselves by encouraging a growth mindset, explaining ADHD, teaching self-regulation and coping skills, and modeling these behaviors themselves.

CHAPTER FIVE

Strengthening Executive Functioning Skills

Parents can help their children with ADHD succeed in social situations, get the help they need, and have a voice in the decisions that affect their lives by fostering in them a strong sense of self-advocacy and assertiveness.

It is crucial for children with ADHD to learn to recognize their strengths and advocate for themselves. Parents can help their children with attention deficit hyperactivity disorder (ADHD) by encouraging a growth mindset, explaining ADHD to them, providing them with tools for self-regulation and coping, and modeling these traits themselves.

Improving Time Management and Organization

Children with ADHD need strong time management and organizational skills to maintain focus, get things done quickly, and meet deadlines. To better manage your time and stay organized, think about the following methods:

- Use visual aids such as calendars, planners, or color-coded schedules to help children visualize and manage their time effectively.

- Break tasks into smaller, manageable steps and teach children how to prioritize and allocate time for each step.

- Establish routines for organizing belongings, such as designated spaces for school supplies, toys, or personal items.

- Teach children strategies for managing distractions, such as creating a quiet workspace or using timers to allocate focused work time.

Children with ADHD can become more productive, less stressed, and more capable of handling their responsibilities by developing and refining their skills in time management and organization.

Enhancing Planning and Problem-Solving Abilities

Children's ability to plan ahead, create strategies, and problem solve are all examples of executive functioning skills. The following methods can help with both planning and problem-solving:

- Teach children how to set realistic goals and break them down into smaller, achievable steps.

- Encourage brainstorming and creative thinking to generate multiple solutions to a problem.

- Help children evaluate the pros and cons of different options and make informed decisions.

- Provide opportunities for children to practice problem-solving in real-life situations, such as resolving conflicts or finding alternative solutions to obstacles.

Young people who are able to plan ahead, formulate strategies, and problem solve effectively have developed crucial executive functioning skills. To better your capacity for planning and solving problems, think about the following:

Developing Task Initiation and Persistence

The ability to get started on a task quickly and keep going until it is finished is what we mean when we talk about task initiation and persistence. Initiating tasks and maintaining concentration are common areas of difficulty for children with ADHD. To improve your ability to start and finish tasks, think about the following techniques:

- Break tasks into smaller, more manageable components to reduce feelings of overwhelm and improve task initiation.

- Use visual or auditory cues, such as timers or alarms, to signal the start or end of a task.

- Set achievable goals and provide regular feedback and reinforcement to maintain motivation and persistence.

- Teach children strategies for managing distractions and maintaining focus, such as creating a designated workspace and practicing attention-focusing exercises.

Children with ADHD can become more proactive, independent learners and increase their overall productivity by practicing task initiation and persistence.

Cultivating Flexibility and Adaptability

Executive functioning skills such as flexibility and adaptability help children deal with change, switch gears, and handle the unexpected. The following methods can help you develop adaptability and flexibility:

- Expose children to new experiences, environments, and challenges to promote adaptability and open-mindedness.

- Encourage children to consider alternative perspectives and approaches to problem-solving.

- Teach children strategies for managing transitions between tasks or activities, such as using visual cues or providing warning signals.

- Foster a supportive and non-judgmental environment where

mistakes are seen as opportunities for learning and growth.

Children with ADHD can develop greater resilience, competence, and openness to transitions and alternative solutions if they are taught to practice flexibility and adaptability.

For children with ADHD to thrive academically, develop emotionally, and live healthy, fulfilled lives, it is essential that their executive functioning skills be bolstered. Parents can help their children with ADHD succeed in many areas by teaching them to better manage their time, organize their belongings, plan ahead, solve problems, stick with tasks, and be more flexible and adaptable.

CHAPTER SIX

Nurturing Social Skills and Relationships

Children with ADHD benefit greatly from the development of strong social skills. Their social and emotional growth depends on their ability to form meaningful connections with others, articulate their needs clearly, and successfully navigate everyday social situations. In what follows, we'll look at some of the ways adults can help kids with ADHD develop their social abilities and friendships.

Understanding Social Challenges Faced by Kids with ADHD

Having trouble with impulse control, hyperactivity, and inattentiveness presents special social challenges for children with ADHD. Parents' awareness of these difficulties and willingness to help is crucial. Think about this:

- Recognize that impulsive behaviors may lead to social misunderstandings or conflicts.
- Understand that difficulties with attention and focus can affect active listening and engagement in conversations.
- Be aware of potential social rejection or isolation that children with ADHD may experience.

Parents can better assist their children with ADHD in social situations if they have a firm grasp of the unique challenges faced by their children.

Teaching Effective Communication Skills

Possessing strong communication skills is essential for making and keeping friends. Children with ADHD can benefit from parental guidance and practice opportunities to help them acquire these skills. Think about implementing these tactics:

- Teach active listening skills, such as maintaining eye contact, asking clarifying questions, and reflecting back what others have said.
- Help children understand the importance of non-verbal cues, such

as body language and facial
expressions, in conveying messages.

- Practice appropriate turn-taking and
  conversational skills, such as waiting
  for a pause before speaking and
  using appropriate tone and volume.
- Role-play social scenarios to help
  children practice assertiveness,
  expressing needs, and resolving
  conflicts.

Parents can help their children with
attention deficit hyperactivity disorder
(ADHD) flourish socially by instructing them
in the art of effective communication.

Promoting Empathy and Perspective-Taking

Children who can empathize with others
and see things from their shoes have a leg

up in the social world. Parents can help their ADHD children develop empathy by using the following methods:

- Model empathy and demonstrate compassion in your own interactions.
- Encourage discussions about different perspectives and feelings in various situations.
- Engage in activities that promote understanding of diverse experiences and cultures.
- Encourage acts of kindness and generosity towards others.

Parents can aid their children with ADHD in making friends and interacting positively with others by encouraging empathy and perspective-taking.

Facilitating Social Connections and Friendships

Children with attention deficit hyperactivity disorder (ADHD) benefit greatly from having strong friendship networks. The following are some ways in which parents can help their children develop their social skills:

- Encourage participation in activities or hobbies where children can interact with peers who share similar interests.

- Facilitate opportunities for socializing, such as playdates, group outings, or joining clubs or teams.

- Provide guidance on appropriate social behaviors, such as taking turns, sharing, and respecting personal boundaries.

- Support the development of social skills by helping children identify and practice appropriate ways to initiate and maintain friendships.

Parents can aid their children with ADHD in these areas by providing opportunities for them to form and maintain friendships, where they can practice and hone their social skills and reap the rewards of genuine human connection.

Children with ADHD benefit greatly from having their social skills and relationships cultivated. Parents can equip their children to successfully navigate social interactions and cultivate meaningful relationships by gaining an understanding of the social challenges their children face, teaching them effective communication skills, encouraging empathy and perspective-taking, and facilitating social connections and friendships.

CHAPTER SEVEN

Managing Emotions and Stress

Children with ADHD often struggle with emotional regulation and stress tolerance. Emotional dysregulation can be exacerbated by impulsivity, hyperactivity, and lack of focus. Parents' guidance and support in developing their children's emotional regulation and coping skills is essential. In the sections that follow, we'll talk about ways to help kids with ADHD deal with their feelings and pressure.

Recognizing and Expressing Emotions

Understanding and communicating feelings are cornerstones of psychological health. Parents can aid their children with ADHD in developing these abilities by providing a loving and accepting home life. Think about implementing these tactics:

Help kids learn to recognize and name their feelings.

It's important to promote honest and non-judgmental conversations about emotions.

Set an example of healthy expression of emotion and acknowledge their feelings.

Methods of expressing feelings should be taught and practiced. These methods include using "I" statements and creative activities like drawing and writing.

Parents can help their children develop emotional intelligence and self-awareness by encouraging them to identify and talk about their feelings.

Coping with Frustration and Impulsivity

Children with ADHD may struggle with frustration and impulsivity. In order to deal with these feelings, they need to learn effective coping mechanisms. Think about implementing these tactics:

- Encourage deep breathing exercises or relaxation techniques to help children calm themselves during moments of frustration or impulsivity.
- Teach problem-solving skills, such as taking a step back, evaluating the situation, and identifying alternative solutions.

- Promote positive self-talk and provide strategies for reframing negative thoughts or challenging situations.

- Help children develop self-control by practicing techniques like counting to ten before responding impulsively.

Parents can help their children with ADHD better regulate their emotions by teaching them coping strategies for dealing with challenging situations.

Stress Management Techniques for Kids with ADHD

Children with ADHD are particularly vulnerable to the negative effects of stress. The best way for children to deal with stress and difficult situations is with the support of their parents. Think about implementing these tactics:

- Encourage physical activities and exercise as a means to release stress and increase endorphin levels.
- Teach relaxation techniques such as progressive muscle relaxation, guided imagery, or mindfulness exercises.
- Encourage the use of creative outlets, such as art, music, or journaling, as a way to express emotions and relieve stress.
- Establish a daily routine that includes dedicated time for relaxation and self-care.

By teaching their children with ADHD stress management skills, parents can help their children develop coping mechanisms that will serve them well throughout life.

Supporting Emotional Regulation and Well-Being

Children with ADHD need help with emotional regulation and general well-being. Parents can foster mental health by creating a warm and accepting home life. Consider the following strategies:

- Establish consistent routines and clear expectations to provide a sense of structure and stability.
- Encourage healthy lifestyle habits, including adequate sleep, balanced nutrition, and regular physical activity.

- Foster positive social connections and opportunities for meaningful relationships.

- Seek professional support, such as therapy or counseling, to help children develop emotional regulation skills.

Parents can help their children with ADHD emotionally by encouraging them to recognize and manage their feelings.

Children with ADHD benefit greatly from learning effective techniques for dealing with stress and negative emotions. Parents can equip their children to deal with emotions and stressful situations by helping them recognize and express their feelings, teaching them strategies for dealing with frustration and impulsivity, providing stress management techniques, and supporting emotional regulation and well-being.

CHAPTER EIGHT

Encouraging Physical Health and Well-Being

Children with ADHD benefit greatly from careful attention to their physical health and well-being. Parents can assist their children in effectively managing ADHD symptoms by emphasizing the importance of exercise, nutrition, sleep, and a balanced lifestyle. In the sections that follow, we'll talk about ways to improve kids with ADHD's health and fitness.

Importance of Exercise and Nutrition

Children with ADHD benefit greatly from regular exercise and a healthy, well-balanced diet. Think about implementing these tactics:

- Encourage physical activities that engage both the mind and body, such as swimming, dancing, martial arts, or team sports.

- Create opportunities for daily exercise, ensuring a mix of aerobic activities, strength training, and flexibility exercises.

- Emphasize the importance of a balanced diet that includes a variety of fruits, vegetables, whole grains, lean proteins, and healthy fats.

- Limit the consumption of processed foods, sugary snacks, and drinks, which can negatively impact attention and behavior.

Children with ADHD greatly benefit from a healthy lifestyle that includes regular exercise and a nutritious diet. Take into account the following options:

Sleep and ADHD: Establishing Healthy Sleep Patterns

The quality and quantity of sleep you get affects your ability to focus, your mood, and your actions the next day. Sleep problems are a common issue for children with ADHD. Think about implementing these tactics:

- Establish a consistent sleep routine by setting regular bedtimes and wake-up times, even on weekends.
- Create a calming bedtime routine that includes activities such as reading, taking a warm bath, or practicing relaxation techniques.

- Create a sleep-friendly environment by ensuring a comfortable bed, minimizing noise and distractions, and maintaining a cool, dark, and quiet bedroom.

- Limit screen time exposure, especially close to bedtime, as it can interfere with sleep quality.

Parents can improve their child's focus, disposition, and health by encouraging regular, restful sleep.

Balancing Screen Time and Other Activities

Children with ADHD need to limit their time in front of screens more than ever before. Long periods of staring at a screen are bad for your health. Think about implementing these tactics:

- Establish clear screen time limits and guidelines that are age-appropriate and tailored to your child's needs.

- Encourage a balance between screen time activities and other activities such as physical play, hobbies, reading, and social interactions.

- Create technology-free zones or times, such as during meals or family gatherings, to promote face-to-face interactions and engagement.

Children with ADHD benefit from participating in a wide range of activities, and parents who encourage a healthy perspective on screen time are better able to facilitate this.

Promoting a Holistic Approach to Health

Taking a holistic view of health requires taking into account the relationship between one's mental, emotional, and physiological states. Think about implementing these tactics:

- Foster open and supportive communication to address the emotional and mental well-being of your child.

- Encourage self-care activities, such as mindfulness exercises, journaling, or engaging in hobbies that bring joy and relaxation.

- Provide opportunities for social interaction and connection with peers, family, and community.

- Seek professional support, such as therapy or counseling, to address any mental health concerns or challenges.

Parents can encourage their child's success in all areas of life by adopting a holistic view of health and wellness for their ADHD child.

Children with ADHD need extra support in maintaining a healthy body and mind. Parental support for their child's physical, mental, and emotional well-being can improve their child's quality of life by prioritizing exercise and nutrition, setting up healthy sleep patterns, striking a balance between screen time, and other activities.

CHAPTER NINE

Celebrating Progress and Resilience

The key to raising strong children with ADHD is to regularly highlight their accomplishments and perseverance. Children with ADHD can benefit from cultivating a growth mindset, building resilience, and providing them with opportunities to experience success on a regular basis. The following sections discuss methods for recognizing and praising children's successes and fortitude while dealing with ADHD.

Recognizing and Acknowledging Achievements

An integral part of nurturing resilient ADHD children is emphasizing their accomplishments and strengths. The development of a positive self-image and motivation in children with ADHD can be aided by recognizing and acknowledging achievements, cultivating a growth mindset, and encouraging resilience in daily life. In the sections that follow, we'll talk about ways to recognize and applaud kids' efforts and perseverance when dealing with ADHD.

- Celebrate both academic and non-academic achievements, such as completing a challenging homework assignment, showing improved self-control, or demonstrating acts of kindness.
- Offer specific praise that focuses on the effort, progress, and strategies

employed rather than solely on the outcome.

- Create a system for tracking and celebrating achievements, such as a sticker chart or a rewards system that aligns with your child's interests and goals.

- Provide verbal affirmations and positive reinforcement to highlight their strengths and accomplishments.

Parents can help their children feel more capable and resilient if they regularly point out and praise their accomplishments.

Cultivating a Growth Mindset in Your Child

A growth mindset is the conviction that one's talents and IQ can be enhanced through sustained and purposeful effort, experience, and the application of one's learned lessons. Young people with attention deficit hyperactivity disorder (ADHD) can benefit from developing a growth mindset. Think about implementing these tactics:

- Encourage your child to embrace challenges as opportunities for growth and learning.
- Teach them that mistakes are an essential part of the learning process and help them reframe setbacks as learning experiences.
- Emphasize the importance of effort, hard work, and persistence in achieving goals.
- Provide constructive feedback that focuses on effort, strategies, and

improvement rather than fixed traits or abilities.

- Encourage them to set realistic and achievable goals, and help them break down larger tasks into smaller, manageable steps.

The ability to accept difficulty, recover quickly from failure, and persevere in the face of adversity can be fostered by teaching children to adopt a growth mindset.

Fostering Resilience in Everyday Life

The capacity to overcome adversity through adaptation, rebound, and flourishing is resilience. Children with ADHD can develop the skills and mindset necessary to deal with adversity by practicing resilience in their daily lives. Think about implementing these tactics:

- Encourage problem-solving skills by helping your child brainstorm solutions, evaluate alternatives, and implement strategies to overcome obstacles.

- Teach them effective coping strategies, such as deep breathing, positive self-talk, and seeking support from trusted individuals.

- Foster a supportive and nurturing environment that encourages open communication, empathy, and understanding.

- Promote self-care activities and healthy outlets for stress relief, such as engaging in hobbies, spending time in nature, or practicing mindfulness exercises.

- Help your child develop a sense of purpose and meaning by encouraging involvement in activities that align with their interests and values.

Parents can equip their children to deal with adversity, embrace change, and develop a growth mindset by modeling these traits in their daily interactions.

Adolescents and young children with attention deficit hyperactivity disorder (ADHD) benefit greatly from hearing positive messages about their achievements and perseverance. Parents can help their children succeed and thrive in the long run by fostering in them a growth mindset, encouraging them to view challenges as opportunities, and praising even the smallest of accomplishments.

CONCLUSION

It takes a multifaceted strategy that takes into account the specific needs of children with ADHD in order to raise them to be resilient. Parents can help their children flourish by providing them with a safe and encouraging home life by implementing the success strategies outlined in this manual.

One of the first steps in helping someone with ADHD is learning about the condition. Parents can better meet their child's needs if they have an understanding of the definition, characteristics, and types of ADHD, as well as the typical difficulties experienced by children with ADHD.

Create a routine, set clear expectations, encourage open lines of communication, be there emotionally, and work together with teachers to make a safe space. These factors improve the health and resilience of children with ADHD by making them feel safe, understood, and supported.

By fostering a growth mindset, explaining ADHD to kids, instructing them in self-control and coping strategies, and encouraging them to be assertive, we can help them become more self-aware and confident. Parents can help their children succeed by giving them the resources they need to learn about and cope with attention deficit hyperactivity disorder (ADHD).

It is crucial to help children with ADHD improve their executive functioning.

Children are better able to overcome obstacles and achieve their goals when they have developed skills in areas such as time management and organization, planning, problem solving, task initiation and persistence, and flexibility and adaptability.

In order to help children with ADHD develop positive social skills and friendships, it's important to first recognize the unique social challenges these kids face and then provide them with the tools they need to overcome them. Parents can help their children with ADHD succeed in social situations by encouraging them to develop their interpersonal skills.

For children with ADHD, emotional and stress management are top priorities. Children can learn to handle their feelings and become more resilient if they practice emotional awareness and expression, develop strategies for dealing with frustration and impulsivity, learn to control their stress, and receive support for their emotional regulation and well-being.

Physical health and well-being can be encouraged by prioritizing physical activity and nutritious eating, establishing regular sleep and wake times, limiting screen time, and engaging in other holistic health practices. Parents can aid their child's growth and resilience by prioritizing their own health.

Finally, a positive self-image and motivation can be fostered in children with ADHD by recognizing and rewarding their efforts to overcome challenges. Children are better equipped to take on challenges, recover from failures, and grow in confidence and resolve when they are regularly reminded of their accomplishments and given praise for overcoming obstacles.

Parents can aid their children who have ADHD in developing resilience and achieving their goals by employing these strategies. Each child is different, so it's important to tailor these methods to their specific requirements. Children with ADHD need parents who are patient, understanding, and committed to their well-being so that they can overcome obstacles, build on their strengths, and find success in their own ways.

THE END